Our Jack Goes West

A Commemorative Novelette

January 28, 1918 - January 28th, 2018

Susan Raby-Dunne

Susan Raby-Dunne

copyright ©2018   ISBN 978-0-9693343-2-3

Published by Bonfire Pictures

P.O. Box 237

Longview, Alberta, CANADA

www.susanrabydunne.com

All rights reserved. No part of this publication may be reproduced, stored in a retrieval system or transmitted in any form, by any process; electronic, mechanical, photocopying, recording or otherwise, without the prior written permission of the copyright holder and Bonfire Pictures.

Lieutenant-Colonel Jack McCrae blows out the lantern and settles into his cot for the night. An asthma attack is trying to build up momentum in his chest and he prays that sleep will overtake him before it can get started. His old enemy hasn't plagued him much over the summer but as fall comes on, here on the French coast with its bone-chilling damp, he knows it will return as always, with a vengeance.

As a last thing, he drops his hand down beside the bed and feels for the top of the dog's head.

"Good-night, Bonneau."

The spaniel's stub of a tail wiggles as McCrae pats him but he doesn't raise his head. Time for quiet and sleep now finally after an exhausting day. Between following Jack through the wards of Number 3 Canadian General Hospital - McGill, on morning and evening rounds, he'd played 'fetch' with two Australian soldiers who never tired of it. One had a crutch and a shattered ankle and the other merely the 'walking pneumonia.'

McCrae on the other hand has spent much of the day treating a continuing flood of casualties from the 3rd Ypres offensive or Passchendaele, as the Canadians call it. The staff were told in advance to evacuate as many patients as possible to make room for the onslaught. He dreads the thought of the damaged men that he knows are coming. Some say it will be worse than the Somme. How could it be worse? He will soon find out as the worst rains in 75 years descend on the low, flat Flanders farmlands.

He didn't even have time for Bonfire today, for his usual evening ride on the big red horse that has been with him since Valcartier, Quebec in 1914, three years ago. The Chestnut Gentleman, as he calls him, has been with him through everything including the terrible battle beside the canal north of Ypres where Lex was killed and where he wrote that indelible poem amidst the carnage and the blood-red poppies.

He was removed from his artillery brigade after that battle under protest, promoted from Major to Lieutenant-Colonel and installed in this war hospital as Doctor in Charge of Medicine.

He refers to Bonfire and dog, Bonneau as *my little family*. Close relationships with human beings have become disappointing, if not painful. It is October of 1917.

As sleep deadens his senses the crunching sound of boots in gravel weaves itself into a dream of moaning men by a road until Bonneau stands and lets out a couple of low *woofs*.

"Jack? Are you awake? Jack?"

McCrae's eyes pop open, instantly furious with this person who would dare interrupt his precious sleep. He swings his legs around and sits on the edge of the bed, plants his feet on the ice-cold wooden floor.

"What is it? Who's there?"

He fumbles for matches and lights the lantern again, hanging it on the centre pole of the tent beside a bloody smock. Bonneau woofs again.

"Birkett," says a man's voice.

McCrae pulls on his trousers, pulls on his boots and changes his attitude. Colonel Herbert Birkett has been the head of the hospital from the beginning. He is respected and well loved.

"Come in, come in, Colonel. What is it? What's wrong?"

Birkett, a short moustached man in his sixties steps into the tiny bell tent and looks around. Shakes his head with a hint of a smile.

"Sorry to disturb you Jack but I'm off tomorrow and I didn't get a chance for a word with you today with all the...with all that new offensive hubbub."

The Colonel is tiny compared to McCrae who is six feet tall.

"Well, what is it Colonel? Please, sit."

The Colonel winces with pain as he slowly lowers himself into the only chair. The condition that is causing his retirement has become acute. McCrae sits on his cot and adjusts a mohair scarf around his neck, tucks it into the neck of his pyjama top again.

"First of all, I'm sorry about the promotion, truly. The decision to pass you over as head was not made lightly."

McCrae waves his hand dismissively. "Elder's clearly the better man."

"No, he's not. Not necessarily. But there's your....." Birkett's voice trails off as he surveys the inside of the bell tent. He sighs and shivers. You can see his breath. McCrae gets an extra army blanket and puts it around the Colonel's shoulders.

"Thank you." Birkett takes a deep breath. "Jack, this is martyr behaviour. There, I've said it." McCrae starts to protest but Birkett silences him with a raised hand. He continues, frustration building. "What have you achieved by refusing more comfortable officer's quarters? By living in this freezing, this blasted bell tent?!"

McCrae looks wounded and wheezes. Birkett notices.

"Listen to yourself! You can't bring back young Lex Helmer by denying yourself...."Birkett is suddenly exhausted and regards McCrae with red, teary eyes. "You can't bring him back. You can't bring back any of them." He slumps back into the chair.

The two men look openly at each other until McCrae's head drops and he stares into his lap. Birkett shifts uncomfortably. Takes another deep breath. "More importantly John Munro Elder is fit Jack and you, are not. With your recurrent respiratory problems, I just couldn't take a chance..."

Now McCrae puts his own hand up in a halt. Birkett falls silent. McCrae closes his eyes and nods. Finally, silently admitting to himself that he's in dreadful physical condition. His cheeks redden. Besides being gassed, some even say he was badly shell-shocked in the battle beside the canal and that he still is. He has wondered that himself.

"I had to tell you these things." There's a brief silence and then Birkett tentatively asks, "May I ask you a favour?"

"Certainly."

"I wondered if you might write me out a copy of the poem. It's very special to me, to all of us, and I'm proud to consider myself a friend of its author."

McCrae nods. He stands and sets the lantern on his tiny writing desk, takes pen and paper out of the drawer. Birkett stands so he can sit down and write. The Colonel stands behind him and places a gentle hand on McCrae's shoulder as he writes out the poem. Moments later McCrae hands the paper to Birkett who holds it up to the lantern.

"Excellent. First rate." He squints at the copy. "In Flanders Fields the poppies blow, between the crosses row on row." He looks up at McCrae. "I shall treasure this. Thank you."

"Say hello to the folks in Montreal for me, will you? I doubt I shall see them again."

"Nonsense! McGill University's favourite pathology professor must return. There will be hell to pay if you don't." Birkett forces a smile.

"Godspeed Colonel and I hope all goes well with the operation. We've all suffered seeing you in such pain."

The two men shake hands emotionally but say nothing more. McCrae watches the older man walk gingerly out the door. He blows out the lantern, undresses and gets back into bed. Seconds later he's asleep, breath rasping loudly in his chest.

* * *

At six a.m. McCrae, still sound asleep, incorporates the actual distant sounds of a ferocious artillery barrage into a repeating dream from his own battle beside the Yser Canal two years ago.

From his dugout in the dyke behind the canal he watches an artillery supply wagon galloping toward him down the Brielen Road toward the crossroads they've named the Devil's Corner. The wagon is heavily laden with 18 pound shells and McCrae knows with absolute certainty that they are about to be blown out of existence by an enemy shell. Then he sees young gunner, Lieutenant Lex Helmer approaching the road from across a field beside it. He tries with all his might to holler out a warning but try as he might, no sound will come out. He's been struck mute.

The shell explodes squarely amidst men and horses and he awakes with a start, sits bolt upright with images of horse and human flesh splattering. That terrible *horse scream* rings in his ears. He sweats, his heart pounds and he now angrily hears the loud peal of bells from the cathedral down the road in the old walled part of Boulogne, in concert with the faint sounds of a barrage somewhere miles away in the Salient. As he tries to calm himself the sight of a concerned Bonneau offers relief.

The dog has been roused by McCrae thrashing about and now rests his head on the bed, looking soulfully into McCrae's eyes. McCrae rolls onto his side and puts his arm around the dog.

The Presbyterian faith that sustained him without question throughout his life has now lost its potency. The only things that now move him through the days are his animal friends and thoughts of those men lost in Flanders. He will carry on for them. That simply is not open to question.

"And you poor beasts that have no choice in the matter. Isn't that right, Bonneau?"

Bonneau's stubby tail wiggles furiously and he answers with a plaintive, "Woo woo wooo."

McCrae can't help but smile. He gives Bonneau a squeeze and tousles his ears. Sits up exhausted, and the smile evaporates as the horse scream still sounds faintly in his head.

The brazier is out and McCrae has a pan of now cold water sitting on it for shaving and washing. Never could abide a moustache. He'd grown one briefly in South Africa when he was a lieutenant at the head of his own artillery section, but the total lack of toilet facilities there or anything one could create to make toilet facilities, like clean water, had made it downright impossible to keep clean. He had shaved it off in disgust one hot, filthy, fly-ridden day in the Karoo. What a relief. He'd never grown another.

* * *

Outside he hears the whistle of an ambulance train arriving from the front. He dresses hurriedly, parts and combs his hair and strides out toward the front of the hospital, the dream finally shaking off in the bracing sea air.

Stretcher bearers are already unloading casualties and as he approaches he hears an orderly with a Yorkshire accent say, "Oh aye, here's one for Colonel McCrae. Came from Doctor… uh, Colonel Davey at No. Canadian C.C.S. Lincolnshire Regiment."

No one here dares call McCrae *Doctor* as a visiting English journalist discovered. McCrae blasted the man, "That is COLONEL McCrae. COLONEL. Do you hear me?"

On the stretcher lies a small, wiry English Tommy with severe and multiple shrapnel injuries and squashed against him, a massive black mongrel dog, its right hind leg mangled with a compound fracture.

A stocky, red-faced stretcher bearer turns to McCrae as he arrives.

"He wouldn't go without the dog, sir. Wouldn't budge without him. Said he'd sooner die, so he did."

"That's alright, Corporal. Bring them in. The pair of them."

Private Will Potter and his dog, Windy have gone 'over the top' three times together with the 1st Lincolns. Windy even has two tiny gold braids on his collar, badges of honour from two previous wounds.

Now the injured pair are on the same bed in Number 3 Canadian General Hospital (McGill) to the consternation of head nursing sister, Matron Katherine MacLatchy. Fortunately for the Tommy and his dog, MacLatchy has a special place in her heart for Jack McCrae, who is allowing this. And McCrae has no end of room in his own heart for dogs, horses and other animals and of course the common fighting soldier. So Will and Windy will stay together, for now at least.

McCrae actually tries to separate them for practical reasons but when the feverish Tommy becomes hysterical, he abandons it.

Matron MacLatchy and the new head of the hospital, Colonel Elder, have already made significant concessions to

McCrae by allowing Bonneau to do rounds with him. They eventually have to admit that it's a terrific tonic for the men in the wards and most of the nursing sisters too, to have the sweet tempered liver and white spaniel nuzzle them and invite their affections. This is a war hospital after all, not Montreal General.

Matron MacLatchy knew McCrae before the war. She tries not to dwell on it. He is simply not the same man now and it's painful to register the change the terrible battle by the canal has wrought in him. He had tried to do some artillery duties when the battle started but was quickly overwhelmed with horrific casualties as only shells and shrapnel can create.

Seventeen straight days of savage fighting and McCrae in an eight by eight foot dirt bunker at the back of the dyke, trying to treat men who had been blown apart by artillery shells. Chlorine gas was used as a weapon by the enemy for the first time in that battle too, and McCrae, already suffering with asthma for many of his forty-two years, was gassed several times.

Seventeen days without a wash, shave or change of clothes, which might have been tolerable if his entire uniform and the tiny bunker had not been soaked with human blood and tissue.

And then the final tragedy; young Lex Helmer, a friend of McCrae's from McGill suffered a direct shell hit and was obliterated. It was in the immediate aftermath during a brief lull in the fighting that the famous poem flowed out, an acceptable way for McCrae to grieve and express his devastation.

Now the Matron watches him attend to Will Potter and his black dog. The spring in his step left him with the first use of gas and death of a friend from home. The soldiers in the wards welcome him with warmth and appreciation. They don't see anything but a kind and attentive doctor. But they did not know him in Montreal.

The one thing that has not left him to the immeasurable benefit of the soldiers, is his bedside manner. Whether it comes naturally to him or is a result of long exposure to the methods of his famous teacher and mentor, Sir William Osler, is a matter for debate among the nursing sisters. Especially among the ones who didn't know him before, when he was jolly and sang in his rich baritone and told endless convoluted and hilarious stories.

MacLatchy believes that in that respect McCrae and Sir William are exactly alike. Like Sir William who affectionately squeezes toes or makes some quip that makes patients forget that the eminent doctor is considered the Father of Modern American Medicine, (even though he's Canadian) McCrae has the same gifted way of connecting with patients, from soldiers to children. Instead of lording over them, as is most often the way with medical men, he puts them at ease, listens to them and more often than not, makes them laugh.

Now as McCrae's vitality ebbs away he is sometimes moody and irritable, even with the sisters or anyone that wastes his time or whines about inconsequential things. MacLatchy literally had to shush him for the first time ever when Queen Mary herself came to inspect the hospital and McCrae launched into a rant about "damn VIPs disrupting his work for no good purpose!" Good Lord, even the Queen herself was not exempt!

But with the death of each soldier Matron MacLatchy can almost see him consciously shepherd his remaining energy and resources to that one purpose, the care of those men.

Sir William Osler's only son, Revere, has recently left a cushy and safe job as quartermaster for the artillery. McCrae has adored Revere since he was born and Revere has long idolized McCrae and was reared on stories of his artillery exploits in the South

African war in 1900. McCrae helped pull all kinds of strings and strokes to get him out of the Medical Corp, and into the artillery.

Sir William has told people privately that, "Long association with Jack McCrae has made Revere a bit bloodthirsty."

This is from a remnant of McCrae the Gunner. The furious McCrae who watched helplessly on the road into Ypres on that spring night of 1915 as the ancient cloth-weaving city was pointlessly battered into rubble by giant shells. As soldiers and even horses fell dead on the cobblestones in front of him having drowned in the throes of asphyxiation from the gas. And he helpless to do a thing for them. Who had ever fought gas?

McCrae had never conceived of such horror when he was tramping around South Africa in 1900; guarding railway lines, taking his artillery column on pointless, wild goose chases without ever laying eyes on the enemy in that vast, mostly empty land. In a letter to his mother on March 18th, 1900 he complained, "Chances of fighting are getting dimmer and more distant and I don't want to return to Canada without a scrap."

This was before the gas and the battle beside the canal. Or July 1st, 1916 when almost 20,000 men were killed in a single day to open the battle of the Somme. In another letter to his mother seventeen years later in the summer of 1917 he would say, "To think of the days when I wanted to be a soldier. Little did I think I would get it in such over-measure."

What most of the people who idolized McCrae the Soldier never knew, including young Revere Osler, is that although he looked for it, he personally saw very little action in the Boer War, only a couple of minor skirmishes. Not enough action to cure him of wanting to see action.

The famous 18th century German military strategist, von Clauswitz said, "The decisive weapon of the future will be massed artillery. This creates a killing ground, (No Man's Land) through which the enemy must advance to seek his own destruction."

This had in fact become the terrible reality of World War One which neither McCrae nor anyone could have conceived of in their worst nightmares.

Matron MacLatchy hopes that McCrae's influence on Revere Osler will not strain his relationship with his mentor. That would be tragic as they had been such great friends over the years. MacLatchy knows that she is not the only one who prays fervently for Revere's safety as he begins his new job with the guns in the Passchendaele offensive.

* * *

So for a couple of days Will Potter and his dog Windy become McCrae's focus and he sets about putting them right. With Windy it's simply a case of anaesthetizing him briefly, setting and putting a cast on his broken hind leg. He's hobbling about quite effectively later that day.

But Will's wounds are severe and complicated; punctured bowel, lacerated liver, partially collapsed lung. The ever-present danger of gas gangrene from the copious manure on the fields of Flanders. No one will baldly come out and say it but McCrae knows that much of that manure is of human origin.

Somehow between surgeons Colonel Elder, Captain Rhea and pathologist, McCrae they patch, clean and stabilize Will Potter. Also knowing that McCrae has Windy on the mend is a tonic for the Private. His gratitude is so effusive that it embarrasses McCrae.

"For Heaven's Sake soldier, it's only a broken leg! It's the least I can do for our four-legged Tommy," as Will thanks him yet again with teary eyes.

Will is stabilized but needs some elaborate, reconstructive surgery if he is to survive and recover and Number 3 Canadian General Hospital (McGill) is simply not equipped to provide it. There's talk now of shipping him home to Blighty to the Royal London Hospital. McCrae knows it must be done but he's already anxious about whether or not the dog will be allowed to go with him. He knows England's animal quarantine rules are strict.

Surely to God they'll make an exception in wartime. Since the battle beside the canal north of Ypres McCrae always feels as though there's a shadow over him anyway, some new source of dread to play on his mind. Like the inexplicable fact the he survived when fully half of his artillery brigade did not. And now it's this. He tries to shut it out of his mind.

In the meantime he's gotten Windy out walking and even attempting to compete with Bonneau in a game of 'fetch the stick.' Bonneau is aloof and not accommodating at all when it comes to fetch. Doesn't give Windy a chance. But at least he tolerates him and doesn't scrap with the canine veteran. Maybe he knows at some level that when Windy does recover, he would not stand a chance agains the bigger and battle-hardened mongrel.

In the hospital Will Potter is sitting up, eating a little but not walking. Until he has the surgery in London, he will be an invalid. McCrae brings Windy in for a visit with his master as often as he dares. Bonneau is tolerated, but McCrae knows two dogs in the ward is pushing it.

A week after Windy and Will's arrival McCrae is taking lunch on the hospital grounds with Windy and Bonneau when the rotund, stubble-faced French caretaker appears carrying two bags of bread and a bottle of milk. He walks toward McCrae and the two dogs. As he gets closer Windy's hair stands up on his back and he produces a low, threatening growl.

McCrae pats his head and says, "Windy, shhh. It's alright. Shush."

But as the janitor passes, Windy, still not too agile with the cast on nevertheless surprises McCrae and the caretaker when he lunges and grabs the pant-leg of the Frenchman, pinching a mouthful of flesh on the back of his calf in the process.

The milk bottle falls on the footpath and shatters, splattering milk all over McCrae and both dogs. Bonneau nonchalantly licks spilled milk off his paws while bread rolls scatter on the ground and McCrae grabs Windy's collar and yanks him back before he can do more damage.

After an initial, "Aaaaoowww," of pain, a barrage of French cursing fills the air with a few English swear words thrown in for good measure. As McCrae struggles to restrain the huge black dog, the Frenchman picks up the scattered rolls stopping at intervals to stab his finger at McCrae and hurl further streams of invective at the three of them.

He foolishly stamps his foot at Windy but Windy is in no way cowed and attempts to lunge at the man again with McCrae hanging on to his collar. The caretaker jumps back in fright but continues to curse at the top of his voice.

Five soldiers lounge on the grass nearby, the two Aussies and three Canucks, and belly-laugh at all this commotion as McCrae tries without success to apologize and placate the Frenchman who now has a trickle of blood staining the back of his pant-leg. He finally gathers up the bread and storms off, still swearing a blue streak.

One of the Aussies who knows Bonneau comes over to help pick up the broken glass from the milk bottle, still stifling laughter. He composes himself.

"Begging your pardon, Colonel, sir," he starts in a heavy Australian accent, "but we heard from a chap in the Lincolns that this old blighter of a dog hates everyone in civvies. Thinks they're bloody...thinks they're slackers, sir." He starts to laugh again.

"Damn it, private," McCrae says sharply. The soldier stops laughing and straightens up. "It's not funny." The two men look at each other and both burst into laughter. McCrae says under his breath, "Never liked that miserable little weasel anyway," upon which they crack up laughing again.

Once the glass is picked up and the Aussie goes back to join his mates, McCrae says to Windy with genuine worry, "Oh, Windy, what are we going to do with you? A dark look comes over him and he shakes his head sadly. "After all your bloody battles dog, this will be your undoing."

In the ward, Colonel Elder has told Will Potter that he is to return to England for surgery and rehabilitation. His days as a frontline soldier are over.

"That's alright, Colonel, that's alright," says Will with a broad smile. "We've given it our best, me and me dog. Me and Windy will make a new life."

Colonel Elder nods and turns away and his heart sinks. Unknown to anyone yet, he has been told by the British *Brass Hats* that due to quarantine regulations, the dog positively will not be allowed to go to England with his master. Not a chance. The kindly Colonel Elder elects not to say a word to Will until he has conferred with McCrae. And he's dreading that conversation too.

* * *

After the terrible battle beside the canal, McCrae was taken out of the artillery very much against his wishes, and transferred to Number 3 Canadian Hospital - McGill. No more soldiering. Only doctoring from then on.

That was bad enough but infinitely worse, he was told that his beloved horse Bonfire would not be coming with him. Medical officers were not allowed horses. This edict was relayed to him by the officious Canadian Surgeon General, G.Carleton Jones, with whom McCrae had bad blood going all the way back to the Boer War. McCrae infuriated Jones in both wars by choosing the artillery over the Canadian Army Medical Corps.

The beautiful red Irish hunter that had come all the way with McCrae from Valcartier, Quebec was going to be reassigned to someone or somewhere else. Who knows? The horse might even end up hauling guns in the field or some other such deadly job. McCrae would not have it. He could not. He thought he would lose his mind when he heard this news.

He immediately set about sending messages to anyone whom he thought would plead his case for keeping Bonfire. Eventually between his close friend, General Morrison who had commanded them in the battle beside the canal, and Canada's eccentric Minister of War, Sam Hughes, the rules were bent and McCrae was allowed to keep his adored equine partner.

So if there is one thing Colonel Elder knows for sure, it is that McCrae will have no end of sympathy for this Tommy that is about to lose his dog. He dreads telling McCrae but knows he will be the best one to break the news to Will Potter.

One day, after a previous long night of surgery, a tall, angular visitor in an American uniform appears outside McCrae's tent. He takes off his cap, puts it back on and takes it off again. He is hesitant to announce himself. Finally he speaks.

"McCrae? You in there? It's Cushing."

"Cushing?" A sleepy McCrae speaks. "Come in." McCrae stretches. "Sorry. Can't wake up. We were at it till two a.m. last night." He stretches again. "What's up?"

Major Harvey Cushing is an eminent neurosurgeon with the Harvard Medical Unit down the road who specializes in removing shrapnel and bullets from soldiers' brains. Cushing and McCrae came to be friends at Johns Hopkins Hospital in Baltimore when McCrae was interning there under Sir William Osler.

When the normally chatty surgeon stands in silence and fidgets with his cap, McCrae sits up suddenly.

"Harvey, what is it? Is something wrong? Is it the Chief?" he asked using the nickname they used for Sir William Osler. McCrae studies Cushing's face, apprehension thick in the air.

"It's Revere. They were up between St. Julien and Langemark...." His voice trails off. McCrae looks at him expectantly until he shakes his head with resignation.

McCrae's face falls. He falls back flat onto the bed and pulls the blanket over his head. Just lies there in shock. Cushing stands in silence. Finally he speaks.

"Jack, I know you're going to blame yourself for steering him into the artillery. You can't. You can't blame yourself for this." Cushing's voice rises in pitch. "Aagh! I knew you'd do this. Revere would not be deterred. You cannot blame yourself for every goddamn thing in this war!"

McCrae lies under the blanket in silence and Cushing storms out of the tent. He stands for a minute, tries to think of something else to say but there is nothing. He says simply, "Shit!" jams on his cap and strides away.

When McCrae emerges a couple of hours later and appears red-eyed and unshaven in the hospital, everyone; Colonel Elder, Matron MacLatchy and all the sisters are on eggshells around him. No idea what, if anything to say. So they say nothing at all.

Colonel Elder had planned to broach the Windy situation this morning and now this. It will have to keep. They still have another day before Will Potter is scheduled to leave.

McCrae is distracted and so gloomy that Elder orders him to take the afternoon off. He goes straight to the barn for Bonfire with Bonneau scampering around him and Windy limping behind. His loyal batman and groom, Dodge brushes and tacks up the horse while McCrae puffs absently on his pipe and the two dogs sit expectantly at his feet.

Private William Dodge has been with McCrae now for almost three years and can read his moods. He also knows that he hasn't smoked a pipe in months. Dodge doesn't know about Revere but he knows well to tread lightly on this day.

He leads a tacked Bonfire out and hands McCrae the reins as McCrae hands him the pipe. Dodge gives him a leg up and he rides away with Bonneau following and Windy limping after. Dodge holds the smouldering pipe and watches him, listens to him coughing .

"Bloody hell," he says, knocking the still burning tobacco out against the heel of his boot. "Bloody hell."

* * *

In the bottom of the Grande Valeé Denacre near the hospital McCrae dismounts and walks along the bramble-lined trail leading Bonfire. It's a hidden world on the edge of the city where McCrae has come with the horse almost every night after work at the hospital. He picks handfuls of blackberries and feeds them to Bonfire who eats them as fast as McCrae can pick them.

It's lush in the valley and heavily shaded, the only sounds being myriad songbirds and the gurgling stream that flows through the mill.

Man and horse walk until they come to the bridge at the mill. McCrae stands on the bridge and loses himself watching the water cascade over the mill wheel. He strokes Bonfire's neck.

"I will only think about this right now. Only this and nothing else."

Later he has a quiet dinner at the Estaminet 2me de Moulin, that is part of the mill. Without much appetite he orders Coq au Vin which he begins to share with the dogs. Jeanne, the matronly cook and wife of the owner comes out of the kitchen with a pot and bowl containing scraps for the the dogs which she sensibly places a distance apart. It's a thoughtful gesture which touches McCrae.

Even Jeanne can see the state of him. For the normally meticulous Colonel to show up in her establishment, unshaven speaks volumes to her. How she despises this war and what it does to people.

It's nearly dark when McCrae returns. Colonel Elder spots him riding toward the barn with no small amount of relief.

* * *

The next day Will Potter is to be put on a Red Cross ship and sail across the channel from Boulogne to England. He keeps asking about Windy. Everyone; doctors, nursing sisters, even other soldiers dodge the question. It seems everyone but Will knows he'll be leaving without the dog.

In the meantime McCrae is pleading with Colonel Elder to appeal for an exception, to no avail. McCrae fails to realize that Elder has already tried his damnedest.

A corporal and sergeant of the Lincolns even try to smuggle Windy on board the ship between blankets on a stretcher but are foiled by a midshipman when Windy thrusts his head out of the blankets and barks at the sailor.

Finally a tearful Will Potter is carried aboard with promises that the dog will be brought to him one way or another. McCrae promises to look after him well in the meantime, and he does.

Windy's leg heals completely and by the onset of winter, he's running alongside Jack and Bonfire, even outpacing the smaller Bonneau. But nothing can cure him of his prejudice against civilians and Jack takes to tying him up outside his tent when he can't supervise him.

When the Canadians finally end the battle of 3rd Ypres by storming Passchendaele Ridge at the beginning of November, the flow of casualties to the hospital increases by hundreds again. McCrae and the entire staff are overwhelmed with the wounded. The injuries from artillery and machine gun fire are horrific. There are also many tales of men with minor injuries that slip into the muck and are unable to free themselves. They sink slowly beneath the yellow mud like quicksand and drown. McCrae cannot even bear to think about the horses and mules lost this way as well.

* * *

In early January McCrae staggers exhausted back to his bell tent after a sixteen hour shift. There's not much fighting at the moment but there are many serious cases of pneumonia, influenza and tuberculosis, all exacerbated by the coldest, wettest winter in decades.

When he arrives at his tent, he finds Windy's empty collar on the ground with the chain still attached. He just stares at it. He's simply too exhausted to look for the dog now. He'll look tomorrow. He retires and slips into unconsciousness the instant his head hits the pillow.

The next morning he awakes to the sound of a dog whining pitifully outside. Sure enough it's Windy. He's lying on his side as rain beats down. McCrae calls him, tries to rouse him but he's unable to get to his feet. McCrae hefts the big dog into his arms and carries him inside. Lays him on a blanket in front of the stove and stokes the fire, throwing in a few chunks of coal that he'd been saving for even colder weather. Snow is predicted.

He examines the dog from head to foot and can't find a mark on him. Every few minutes Windy yelps. Then he starts to pant. Then he vomits several times. Although the substance doesn't look unusual, McCrae notices a metallic odour coming from it. He sends Dodge to find Captain Rhea and Colonel Elder for their opinions. Colonel Elder is in surgery so Dodge comes back with Rhea, a Texas transplant who had gone to Montreal to study medicine at McGill and has ended up here in the war hospital as a surgeon.

McCrae takes morphine ampules out of his bag. He can't bear to see the dog in such pain. Rhea stands and looks down at the dog.

"I'd say poison," Rhea say matter-of-factly with his soft Texas drawl. "That French caretaker's been gunnin' for him since he got bit. Rat poison, or maybe strychnine. You better face it, Jack, he's a gonner. This dog's a' goin' west."

McCrae sits in front of the stove with Windy's head on his lap for the next few hours. Whenever the pain returns, he gives him more morphine. There's nothing else to be done.

They bury Windy on the hospital grounds with a little wooden cross to mark the spot. They give his collar, now with three gold braids to signify his war wounds, to the 1 Lincolns.

* * *

On the afternoon of January 22nd, 1918, Matron Katherine MacLatchy walks by the officer's mess and does a double take when she sees Jack McCrae asleep in a chair. She stands above him. His chin rests on his chest and his breath rasps in and out. He's in a profound sleep.

"My word," she says to herself, "this is not like him. Not like him at all." Matron MacLatchy has a simple rule for her charges, whether they be children, family or even dogs and horses; *When they don't do what they always do, something is wrong.*

The Matron squeezes McCrae's shoulder and he slowly looks up at her bleary-eyed, uncomprehending.

"Colonel? Are you alright?"

Recognition comes into his eyes. He looks around the mess.

"Hmm. Must have fallen asleep. What time is it?"

"Two-thirty," says the Matron.

He looks alarmed. "In the morning?"

"No, Jack, it's the middle of the afternoon."

"You don't say." He looks around the room again. "Actually, I've got a splitting headache."

The Matron puts her hand on his forehead.

"You're a little warm. Not bad though. Anyway, I think you should get into bed. And not in that godforsaken tent," she says sternly.

"I'll be fine," says McCrae getting unsteadily to his feet.

"Tch. Jack McCrae, if I have to get Colonel Elder to pull rank and order you to stay inside, in proper officer's quarters, I will. You are staying inside, in a proper room with a proper bed where I can keep an eye on you."

McCrae studies her for a few seconds but thinks better of challenging her. Birkett was the last hospital head replaced by Elder but everyone knows who *really* runs the place and he's looking at her.

"Alright," he concedes, "but just for tonight."

MacLatchey gets him into a room reserved for officers and offers to make him a cup of tea, which he accepts. When she returns a few minutes later, he has lapsed into deep sleep again. She sets the tea down and listens to his breathing. His breath rasps and crackles in his chest. She can't decide if it's his normal asthma or something new.

Outside she quietly closes the door and promptly bursts into tears. She wipes her eyes impatiently. "For pity sake MacLatchy, pull yourself together." She looks around furtively and hopes no one has seen this unseemly outburst.

Later that evening, MacLatchy comes into McCrae's room with soup and tea. She finds him sitting up and reading and is relieved to see it although he has a bad cough and she doesn't like his colour.

"I'm glad you're awake because we have news." Matron MacLatchy beams. McCrae sets down his book.

"We?" he asks. It's then he sees the great hulking form of Colonel John Elder behind her in the doorway as she places the tray on his lap. He nods a greeting to Elder, and then speaks to the Matron. "No soup, thanks. But I'll have the tea. What's the news?"

Colonel Elder shifts his bulk into the small room. "Jack, how are you feeling?"

"I've been better, John. But I'll live." He manages a weak smile. "Now, what have you got to tell me?"

Elder unfolds a piece of yellow paper an clears his throat. "This is to notify Lieutenant-Colonel John McCrae that he is appointed and to be dispatched immediately as Consulting Physician to the British First Army." Elder looks up from the paper with a big smile.

Matron MacLatchy speaks. "We'll hate to lose you, Jack but my word, what an honour. And for a Canadian to boot. We're all very proud of you Jack McCrae."

McCrae looks pleased and leans back against his pillows. "Well. Well well. It's not quite back to the front. But it's closer to the fight than this."

Matron shakes her head and says, "Phfftt."

"It's a happy and prestigious compromise, and one where you're less likely to be killed," says Colonel Elder. He walks over and the two men shake hands. "Congratulations, Colonel McCrae."

"Now, we'll leave you to your rest. Can I get you anything else?" says the Matron. She looks at the untouched soup. "I wish you'd eat something. Is your stomach not well?"

"I'm fine Katherine. I'll be fine. Thanks." McCrae waves the Matron and the Colonel out of the room. "You two have needier patients than me. Now off you go."

* * *

The next morning Matron MacLatchy looks in on McCrae and is alarmed when she sees him. He's turned a dusky colour and breathes in short rasps. She takes his temperature and it has shot up to 102 degrees. She works at seeming unconcerned.

" Has it gone up?" he asks weakly.

"A little," she says. "Must be flu, I think."

That afternoon they have McCrae on a stretcher and load him into an ambulance truck for the British Officers Hospital down the road in Wimereux. They want him to have the best possible care. Matron MacLatchy, Colonel Elder and Captain Rhea stand and fret in silence as the ambulance drives away. No one wants to share what they are thinking.

Sometime after midnight, Private Dodge cleans Bonfire's stall. He can't sleep with worrying. Bonfire stands quietly in the corner as Dodge works around him with the pitchfork.

"Might as well muck your stall, Master Bonfire. Can't bloody well sleep anyway. And I don't need the Colonel getting after me about the state of your lodgings when he gets home do I?"

Suddenly Bonfire raises his head. With ears perked expectantly, he turns toward the stall door and takes a couple of steps. He looks over the half door and down the barn aisle to the main barn door. Nickers softly, or as McCrae calls it, *whickers*. That soft, endearing sound a horse makes to greet a friend or when expecting a treat.

Dodge stops mucking and stands beside Bonfire. He looks down the aisle too. No one is there. Dodge takes out his pocket watch and notes the time. 1:30 a.m. He looks at the horse and sighs sadly. Strokes Bonfire's neck.

Not daring to speak above a whisper he says, "I'm…I'm afraid he's gone old son."

Five o'clock in the morning Colonel Elder and Dodge stand in the hall beside the phone. Elder adjusts his glasses and dials as Dodge looks on hopefully.

"How is he," asks the Colonel. His head drops. "I see. When? Yes, thank you. I'll notify everyone."

Dodge looks at Colonel Elder expectantly.

"He's gone, Dodge. Pneumonia, meningitis, paralysis."

Dodge turns away as his eyes fill with tears. Puts his cap on and starts to walk. He stops and turns around again.

"Colonel?" Dodge takes his cap off again.

"Yes, Dodge." Colonel Elder's voice cracks and his eyes brim with tears.

"When was it? When did he die?"

"1:30 this morning."

Dodge puts on his cap and walks out. "Gone west with all the good 'uns," he says sorrowfully.

* * *

January 29th, 1918 is an unseasonably warm day in Wimereux on the coast of France. The sun brightly glints off the ocean and a warm wind blows. Over the hill from the town comes a huge procession led by chief mourners, Matron MacLatchy and Sir Bertrand Dawson from the British Officer's Hospital.

They are followed by Colonel Elder and six sergeants carrying Jack McCrae in a flag-draped coffin. Directly behind the casket Dodge leads Bonfire with McCrae's boots reversed in the stirrups. It is to be one of the biggest funerals ever in World War One.

Over five hundred people attend the funeral of the beloved soldier/poet including Canadian Corps commander, General Arthur Currie and McCrae's best friend, General Edward Morrison. Major Harvey Cushing leads a contingent from the Harvard Hospital.

Cushing whispers to a colleague, "He was a soldier from top to toe. How he would have hated to die in bed!"

Colonel Elder abruptly covers his face with his cap, his great shoulders shaking. Captain Lawrence Rhea dabs at his eyes behind spectacles. The nursing sisters weep openly.

With reversed arms, soldiers of the Stafford Regiment, rather than fire over the grave as is the tradition in peace time, stand at salute. A lone soldier plays The Last Post on his bugle and as the coffin is lowered, artillery guns sound distantly in the Salient as though cued by the gunner's last moments above ground.

* * *

Late that evening in the barn, Bonfire's stall is empty. The barn door is open and there's a hollow clopping of horse's hooves on cobblestones. Dodge runs with Bonfire in hand. He is taking the horse to a secret, prearranged place where he hopes the horse will live out his years in peace. Loyal to the end, he will not have McCrae's beloved horse pressed into service hauling guns or supply wagons.

* * *

In Montreal Colonel Birkett is recovering well from his surgery when he receives a long letter from Colonel Elder dated February 1st, 1918. He knows of the death of McCrae from a telegram but this is a blow by blow of the events leading to the death of an icon. He makes a cup of tea first and sits down, braced for the details.

Birkett reads the first part of the letter with relative detachment; loss of appetite, slightly elevated temperature, normal pulse and respirations. "Mm hmm, mm hmm." As he reads, he knows at some level that his thinking is magical and in the back of his mind, he is still hoping against hope that the letter will say ultimately that all is well. That McCrae is recovering and there is nothing to worry about.

He holds it together until Elder speaks of a remarkable change that takes place in the early hours of January 28th. McCrae has suddenly developed paralysis on his right side, Bell's palsy on his face although he is totally unconscious, and he is in fact dying with a pulse too faint to count.

His breath catches in his throat as he reads Elder's final words; "This is a correct diary of the awful tragedy that has come upon us, and I cannot, even yet, realize that I shall never see Jack again."

Birkett sets the letter down and sobs from the depths of his soul. He sobs not just for Jack McCrae but for all of it; all the terrible loss and events of four years of war.

Once he has composed himself, he shuffles to his writing desk and opens a drawer. He pulls out a manilla envelope. Inside the envelope and protected between two sheets of cardboard he slides out a treasured piece of paper with handwriting on it. He hasn't looked at it since he left Boulogne. Actually, since it was handed to him. Now seems like an appropriate time. He composes himself, clears his throat and reads…

In Flanders Fields

In Flanders fields the poppies blow,

Between the crosses, row on row,

That mark our place; and in the sky

The larks, still braving singing, fly

Scarce heard amid the guns below.

We are the Dead. Short days ago

We lived, felt dawn, saw sunset glow,

Loved and were loved, and now we lie

In Flanders fields.

Take up our quarrel with the foe:

To you from failing hands we throw

The torch; be yours to hold it high.

If ye break faith with us who die

We shall not sleep, though poppies grow

In Flanders Fields

Note: For dramatic purposes, some events are out of sequence.

Back photo - John McCrae, 1914 - University of Victoria

John McCrae's grave - Susan Raby-Dunne

Cover design - Angela Simmons

www.susanrabydunne.com

www.canadianwarhistorytours.com

The author in Adegem Canadian Military Cemetery, Adegem, Belgium.

January 28, 2018 marks 100 years since John McCrae died. After studying his life for thirteen years, my fascination continues and I keep learning new things. What he did in life, and his indelible poem, *In Flanders Fields*, still matters. He is still loved, and not forgotten.

www.ingramcontent.com/pod-product-compliance
Lightning Source LLC
Chambersburg PA
CBHW050608300426
44112CB00013B/2125